DEALING WITH
**MENTAL
DISORDERS**

DEALING WITH

BIPOLAR
DISORDER

By Melissa Abramovitz

ReferencePoint
Press®

San Diego, CA

© 2020 ReferencePoint Press, Inc.
Printed in the United States

For more information, contact:
ReferencePoint Press, Inc.
PO Box 27779
San Diego, CA 92198
www.ReferencePointPress.com

ALL RIGHTS RESERVED.

No part of this work covered by the copyright hereon may be reproduced or used in any form or by any means—graphic, electronic, or mechanical, including photocopying, recording, taping, web distribution, or information storage retrieval systems—without the written permission of the publisher.

Content Consultant: Carla Marie Manly, PhD

LIBRARY OF CONGRESS CATALOGING-IN-PUBLICATION DATA

Names: Abramovitz, Melissa, 1954– author.
Title: Dealing with bipolar disorder / Melissa Abramovitz.
Description: San Diego, CA : ReferencePoint Press, 2020. | Series: Dealing with mental
    disorders | Includes bibliographical references and index. | Audience: Grades 10-12.
Identifiers: LCCN 2019034020 (print) | LCCN 2019034021 (eBook) | ISBN 9781682827871
    (hardcover) | ISBN 9781682827888 (eBook)
Subjects: LCSH: Manic-depressive illness--Juvenile literature.
Classification: LCC RC516 .A2824 2020 (print) | LCC RC516 (ebook) | DDC 616.89/5--dc23
LC record available at https://lccn.loc.gov/2019034020
LC ebook record available at https://lccn.loc.gov/2019034021

CONTENTS

THE CHALLENGES OF BIPOLAR DISORDER

Jamie was eleven years old when she began experiencing intense mood swings and hearing voices inside her head telling her that people were trying to kill her. Sometimes she felt so sad that she cried uncontrollably for hours. Then, she suddenly raced through the house, talking or screaming nonstop, throwing and breaking things.

Before Jamie turned twelve, she was confined to a psychiatric hospital ten times and received four different diagnoses. Finally, a psychiatrist who observed her behavior for several months told her parents she had bipolar disorder (BD). He believed the other psychiatrists had misdiagnosed Jamie because symptoms in children and adolescents with BD differ from those in adults. This doctor started Jamie on two medications used to treat BD, but they made her nauseous. He tried other drugs, and after months of adjusting Jamie's dosages, her extreme mood swings from mania to depression—hallmarks of BD—became less drastic.

Hallucinations can be a symptom of bipolar disorder. Diagnosing bipolar disorder in children can be more difficult than in adults because the diagnostic criteria are different.

Jamie finally went home to live with her family. During her teen years, however, she rebelled by refusing to take her medications. She also started abusing marijuana and cocaine. Finally, her two best friends told her they were tired of her outbursts and risky behavior. Jamie realized she had to take responsibility for helping herself live successfully with the disorder. She began seeing a psychiatrist and a psychotherapist regularly and took her medications as prescribed. She started studying instead of getting high, and her grades improved so much that she was accepted at a top university. Her friends became her staunch allies again.

The fear of stigma can make it hard for a person to seek treatment for bipolar disorder. Co-occurring disorders and misdiagnosis are also barriers to treatment.

Jamie is a fictional character whose behaviors and experiences represent a composite of real people with BD. Her story illustrates how challenging dealing with every aspect of BD is for patients, their families, and the health care professionals who treat the illness. Although anyone of any age can develop BD, it is a lifelong, or chronic, disorder. Mental health writer and patient advocate Marcia Purse, who has BD, notes that this makes the "emotional, practical, and social challenges" ongoing.[1]

CHALLENGES IN DIAGNOSING, TREATING, AND LIVING WITH BIPOLAR DISORDER

Jamie's long road to receiving a correct diagnosis and treatment regimen is not uncommon. This results from the fact that many people with BD have other mental disorders such as obsessive-compulsive disorder (OCD) and attention-deficit/hyperactivity disorder (ADHD). This complicates diagnosis and treatment. As the National Alliance on Mental Illness (NAMI) explains, "[T]he antidepressants used to treat OCD and the stimulants used to treat ADHD may worsen symptoms of bipolar disorder and may even trigger a manic episode."[2] Doctors must therefore prescribe medications that do not worsen co-occurring disorders once they diagnose these disorders.

Another major challenge in living with BD is the stigma related to serious mental illnesses. Stigma refers to unfavorable perceptions and prejudices held by many people in society. Stigma toward people with mental illness has existed throughout history. Many patients say it is hurtful and leads to shame in individuals and families. Gabe Howard, a person with BD, writes that stigma leads to misconceptions that "can slowly chip away at someone's self-worth and confidence." In addition, he states, "People tend to make blanket assumptions about my life based on a lot of false stereotypes surrounding bipolar disorder and those of us who live with it. People believe we are unable to work, can't be in stable relationships, and must live off our parents, among other things."[3] Gabe, like many others with BD, has a good job, works hard, owns his home, is married, and adores his puppy. Many patients and families say combating stigma is among the most challenging aspects of living with the disorder.

> "People tend to make blanket assumptions about my life based on a lot of false stereotypes surrounding bipolar disorder and those of us who live with it. People believe we are unable to work, can't be in stable relationships, and must live off our parents, among other things."[3]
>
> – Gabe Howard, a person with bipolar disorder

It is possible to treat and manage bipolar disorder. Through a combination of therapy and medications, many people maintain a good quality of life.

HOPE FOR MILLIONS WITH BIPOLAR DISORDER

The millions of people affected by BD hope increased awareness about the disorder and the people who have it will decrease stigma. In turn, they hope this will make others with BD more willing to seek diagnosis and treatment. They also hope ongoing research will lead to a better quality of life for people with BD. However, these challenges do not affect only the estimated 4.4 percent of American adults who will experience bipolar disorder at some point in their lives. BD affects families and societies throughout the world. The World Health Organization (WHO) estimates 60 million people worldwide have the disorder.

BD imposes many costs on society. Many families face economic hardship and even bankruptcy because of astronomical medical costs, so taxpayers end up paying these costs. Taxpayers also pay for expenses associated with crimes committed by and against people with BD. Additional costs to society come from the fact that many people with BD are unable to work. A 2016 study by researchers at Oxford University found that BD "is one of the leading causes of disability worldwide and is associated with significant direct and indirect costs."[4] Direct costs include costs for medication, psychotherapy, and hospitalizations. Indirect costs affect society when people with BD cannot work to support themselves. The researchers found that each patient generates more than $160,000 in expenses to families and society during his or her lifetime.

BD affects individuals, families, and society. Its wide reach underlies efforts by mental health advocates and biomedical researchers to improve patients' access to useful information, knowledgeable health care providers, and effective treatments. In their book *Manic-Depressive Illness*, whose title uses an old name for BD, psychiatrists Frederick K. Goodwin and Kay Redfield Jamison convey the universality and shared burden of BD in their characterization of its main features: "Manic-depressive illness magnifies common human experiences to larger-than-life proportions."[5]

"Manic-depressive illness magnifies common human experiences to larger-than-life proportions."[5]

– Psychiatrists Frederick K. Goodwin and Kay Redfield Jamison

CHAPTER
ONE

WHAT IS BIPOLAR DISORDER?

The National Institute of Mental Health (NIMH) says that bipolar disorder creates "unusual shifts in mood, energy, activity levels, and the ability to carry out day-to-day tasks."[6] NIMH emphasizes that these shifts are far more extreme than the normal changes that everyone experiences. The intensity of these shifts is what makes BD a disorder.

MAIN CHARACTERISTICS

The primary hallmark of BD is the shift between two emotional states, or poles. People with BD experience periods of mania. Mania is a period of high-spiritedness or irritability accompanied by other symptoms, such as racing thoughts and engaging in risky behavior. Depressive episodes often follow, though they are not required for diagnosis. This characteristic shift in mood is why the name is now bipolar disorder. In contrast, major depressive disorder does not involve mania. For a diagnosis of bipolar disorder, behavior must significantly impair the ability of a patient to function at work or in society. In addition, manic and depressive episodes must not be attributable to medication or other substances.

Bipolar disorder is characterized by shifts between mania and depression. While depressive episodes are not required for a diagnosis, they are common for people with bipolar disorder.

The nature of the manic and depressive cycles is different in different people and can change in the same individual over time. Episodes can last for minutes, hours, days, weeks, or months, and the length of time between episodes can range from seconds to years. Some patients experience few or no symptoms in between major episodes, while others have continuous symptoms and associated difficulties. Some experience what health care providers call rapid cycling. This means episodes do not last long and quickly shift from extreme highs to extreme lows, sometimes many times each day. Some have mixed states, which means they experience elements of mania and depression at the same time.

The average age at which BD begins is twenty-five. However, it can start in people of any age and affects people of all races, ethnicities, and social classes worldwide. Studies indicate that the majority of cases— from 50 percent to 66 percent—begin before age nineteen, and doctors have diagnosed BD in children as young as five. In general, the earlier the disorder begins, the more severe it is, and the more likely the individual is to experience rapid cycling and to engage in self-harm or suicide as an adult. No matter when BD begins, it is chronic.

COMMON SYMPTOMS

Symptoms vary among individuals, but they all involve a departure from an individual's normal behavior. Common symptoms during mania include extremely high energy, elevated mood, inflated self-esteem, little need for sleep, flight of ideas, and engaging in risky behavior. Other indicators are being more talkative than normal and being distractible. In some patients, mania includes irritability and agitation. John, a psychiatrist with BD, says his manic episodes are "like being taken, against my will, to a place of insanity where I lose my moral compass."[7]

Symptoms during depressive episodes include depressed mood, loss of interest in activities, decreased appetite or weight loss, loss of energy, feelings of worthlessness or unnecessary guilt, thoughts of suicide, and either an inability to sleep or a compulsion to sleep most of the time. Many people with severe depression cannot even get out of bed and think constantly about death or their own perceived worthlessness. Psychiatrist Kay Redfield Jamison experienced her first breakdown due to BD at age seventeen. She wrote that during the depression that followed

In order for behavior to be manic, it must be different from the person's usual behavior. Compulsive shopping or overspending by a normally careful shopper may be a sign of a manic episode.

her manic exuberance, her mind "mocked me for my vapid enthusiasms; it laughed at all of my foolish plans; it no longer found anything interesting or enjoyable or worthwhile."[8]

Another symptom of BD may include psychosis. People with psychotic symptoms have delusions (false beliefs) and hallucinations (false sensory perceptions, such as hearing imaginary voices) that they believe are true, real-life experiences. In these patients, delusions and hallucinations tend to reflect their current mood extreme. Those experiencing mania may believe they have special powers, are a messenger from God, or are a famous person. During depression, psychotic symptoms often center on darkness and fear. A patient may think she is a grotesque monster or a cadaver. Linda Logan, a young mother of three children, thought she was no longer human. She described herself as "black vermicelli on an asphalt driveway." In another delusion, she could not distinguish herself from her surroundings. "My sense of boundedness—where I stopped and other people or the environment began—was sloppy, like a toddler scribbling outside the lines," she explained.[9]

> "My sense of boundedness–where I stopped and other people or the environment began–was sloppy, like a toddler scribbling outside the lines."[9]
>
> *– Linda Logan, a person with BD*

Some people with BD are violent. This most commonly occurs during manic episodes that include irritability and agitation. These negative consequences often arise as a result of poor judgment, lack of insight, and hyperactivity associated with manic episodes. It may happen when delusions convince the person that others seek to harm him. It could also result when imagined voices command him to harm or kill someone. People with BD are also far more likely to attempt or complete suicide than the general population. Suicide attempts and completions can occur during manic or depressive episodes.

Most of the time, symptoms emerge gradually, but many people do not notice these symptoms unless and until they become extreme. Once they appear, symptoms may shift rapidly. In many cases, people start to feel energetic and positive when manic episodes occur before depressive ones. They may soon need less and less sleep, which can be an indicator of an oncoming manic episode.

Mania can cause people to behave violently. Irritability is a common symptom of mania.

There is another level of mania known as hypomania. Hypomania is similar to mania, but less severe. Sometimes hypomanic episodes are the only mania a person experiences. But most cases progress to full-blown mania. Crushing depression often follows. Sometimes this occurs soon after episodes of mania, but sometimes depression does not emerge for years. The opposite may also be true.

SYMPTOMS IN CHILDREN

Symptoms in children and adolescents are usually different from those in adults and require special considerations before making a formal diagnosis. "Onset of bipolar disorder during childhood and adolescence appears to be a more severe form of bipolar than adult onset and there tends to be more psychosis involved," states the

Medifocus Guidebook on: Bipolar Disorder. "Children and adolescents also tend to experience very rapid mood swings many times a day. . . . It is common to see children experience depressive states in the morning that [are] followed by increasing energy and mania later in the afternoon or evening."[10] Children with BD are also likely to have no symptom-free breaks after episodes, and they tend to have frequent, explosive temper tantrums and to cry for hours on end.

"Onset of bipolar disorder during childhood and adolescence appears to be a more severe form of bipolar than adult onset and there tends to be more psychosis involved."[10]

– Medifocus Guidebook on: Bipolar Disorder

In some children, symptoms become less extreme as they mature. In others, especially in those who receive no treatment, symptoms remain severe throughout their lives. Some cases that start in childhood or adolescence begin with fairly mild symptoms that worsen over time. Kay Jamison, for example, experienced her first manic episodes at age seventeen and found them exhilarating. "At first, everything seemed so easy," she later wrote. "I raced about like a crazed weasel, bubbling with plans and enthusiasms, immersed in sports, and staying up all night, night after night, out with friends, reading everything that wasn't nailed down." Soon, however, the episodes included frightening hallucinations and delusions that were "psychotically out of control."[11]

Some behaviors or falsehoods in children with BD are appropriate to the child's age. For example, a nine- or ten-year-old might tell his family he is smarter than his teacher at school. But other times, children act inappropriately for their age. Some flirt with adults or try to touch other people's genitals. Many also get far less sleep than other children, getting just three or four hours a night. A key factor is that this is a change from the child's normal behavior.

WHAT CAUSES BD?

Modern experts believe BD is caused by complex interactions between genetics, behavioral and environmental factors, and abnormalities in the structure and function of the brain. The fact that BD runs in certain families demonstrates that genetics is one underlying cause. In fact, genes are the greatest risk factor. "Twin studies have established that bipolar disorder is among the most heritable of medical disorders," write neuroscientists Jennifer H. Barnett and Jordan W. Smoller.[12] Twin studies look at both identical twins, who share the same genes, and fraternal twins, who usually share half of their genes. Such studies show that if one twin in a pair of identical twins has BD, the other twin develops the disorder about 39 to 43 percent of the time. The rate for fraternal twins, by contrast, was 4.5 to 5.6 percent. This shows that genetics are part of the cause of bipolar disorder. However, the fact that both identical twins do not always develop BD indicates that factors besides genes play a role in causing it.

> "Twin studies have established that bipolar disorder is among the most heritable of medical disorders."[12]
>
> – Neuroscientists Jennifer H. Barnett and Jordan W. Smoller

Genes are DNA molecules that encode and transmit hereditary information from parents to their offspring. For instance, a person's eye color is a trait that can be traced to their genes. Genes reside on strands of DNA called chromosomes, which are located in the center, or nucleus, of each body cell. Genes use RNA molecules to translate and transmit their encoded instructions to cell parts that carry out these instructions.

Health care professionals think genetics could be a cause of BD. But there are other causes as well.

Gene abnormalities, also known as mutations, can cause disease by encoding and transmitting faulty instructions that lead to abnormal structure or activity in body parts. The faulty instructions from gene mutations that underlie BD can cause abnormalities in how brain cells communicate and are put together into brain structures.

The main parts of neurons are the cell body, axons, and dendrites. The cell body contains the genetic material, DNA, in its nucleus. Axons are long extensions from the cell body that transmit chemical and electrical signals to other neurons. These signals travel across tiny gaps between neurons called synapses. These signals are received by receptors on other neurons' short extensions, or dendrites. Each neuron's receptors are designed to take up specific brain chemicals used in communication.

These chemicals are called neurotransmitters. Defects in the receptors, other cell parts, synapses, neurotransmitters, or the mechanisms by which these structures operate can cause disorder.

Gene mutations can cause a disease directly or by making a person more likely to develop it. For example, a mutation of the CFTR gene directly causes cystic fibrosis. Children who inherit this gene mutation always develop the disease. In contrast, mutations in many genes give people a predisposition, meaning an increased risk, for developing BD. This means the individual will not develop BD unless certain behaviors or environmental factors are also present.

Researchers have identified many abnormal genes that contribute to the predisposition for BD. They do this by studying sequences of gene patterns that recur in people with the disorder. They then compare these sequences to the DNA of people without BD.

One gene connected to BD is SLC6A4, which regulates the serotonin transporter protein. Serotonin is a neurotransmitter that stabilizes mood and regulates sleep, among other functions. The serotonin transporter protein carries serotonin from synapses to neurons. These neurons' receptors bind to the serotonin and re-release it to other neurons. Mutations in this gene can disrupt these processes and produce symptoms of BD.

Mutations in the CLOCK genes also contribute to BD. These genes control a group of cells in the brain called the suprachiasmatic nucleus, also known as the internal biological clock that regulates sleep-wake cycles. Neuroscientists believe CLOCK gene mutations underlie the sleep-wake abnormalities in BD. They are believed to be the reason that

GENETIC LINKS BETWEEN BD, SCHIZOPHRENIA, AND AUTISM

A study reported in March 2018 by a team of researchers at the University of California, Los Angeles, revealed that people who had bipolar disorder, schizophrenia, or autism during their lifetime shared many of the same gene mutations. The researchers examined the DNA and brains of deceased people who had these disorders and found that the same gene mutations can lead to different brain abnormalities that underlie different mental disorders. This occurs because the genes can be expressed differently in different people. Gene expression refers to how the instructions encoded by genes are carried out by the body.

Regulatory DNA is involved in gene expression. Located between genes, its main function is to turn genes on or off. Genes that are turned off do not perform their assigned duties at all, and genes that are turned on sometimes send distorted instructions that result in cells producing abnormal substances or engaging in unusual activities. All of these genetic flaws can lead to characteristic symptoms of bipolar disorder, schizophrenia, or autism, depending on which genes are expressed.

insufficient sleep can trigger bipolar episodes. Researchers believe many more genes contribute to BD. They continue to search for more of these genes in the hope that this will lead to new insights about the disorder.

BRAIN ABNORMALITIES

Abnormal genes contribute to the problems with the brain's structure that underlie BD. The brain's structure consists of four main sections, or lobes. They are the frontal, parietal, occipital, and temporal lobes. The outer layer of cells around these lobes comprises the cerebral cortex, which is the area responsible for higher thinking functions such as reasoning, memory, and decision-making. Different areas of the cortex perform different functions. For example, the prefrontal cortex is important in planning, decision-making, and regulating activity in brain areas that deal with emotion. Underneath the cortex are numerous structures that are essential for relaying information to the cortex and coordinating the complex connections that control sensory perception, movement, and other functions.

Doctors detect brain abnormalities using computerized tomography (CT), magnetic resonance imaging (MRI), functional magnetic resonance imaging (fMRI), and positron emission tomography (PET) imaging technologies. CT uses X-rays, and MRI uses radio waves and magnetic fields to create detailed computerized cross-sectional images of brain structures. FMRI uses MRI technologies to measure activity in certain brain areas. One way in which it detects this activity is by measuring blood flow in the area. PET scans use radioactive tracer dye that doctors inject into patients' blood vessels to detect and measure both structure and activity in the brain. PET detects the energy the tracer dye produces and sends this information to a computer. The computer converts the information into three-dimensional pictures of brain structures. This technology measures brain activity using blood flow, oxygen use, and cell metabolism.

These imaging tests indicate that people with BD have numerous abnormalities in brain areas that regulate emotion, mood, sleep, and self-control. One structural abnormality that underlies the emotional and cognitive defects in people with BD is decreased size and fewer than normal neurons in the anterior cingulate cortex, which is involved with attention, decision-making, emotion, and memory.

Studies by researchers with the Heinz C. Prechter Bipolar Research Program at the University of Michigan, Ann Arbor, shed light on how some defects that underlie BD start to develop early on in brain growth. They found that neurons in the developing brains of fetuses, as well as neurons in children with gene mutations that increase the risk of BD, are

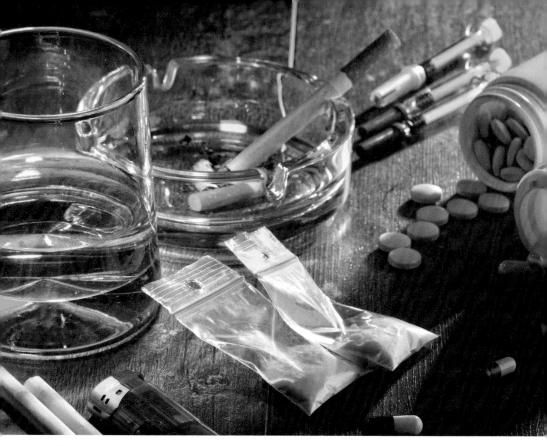

Substance abuse and trauma increase a person's risk of developing bipolar disorder. Certain drugs and alcohol can also make bipolar disorder worse for those who already have it.

improperly "addressed . . . like misdirected letters and packages at the post office," and end up settling in different areas of the brain compared with similar neurons in normally developing brains.[13] How these errors help cause BD is as yet unknown.

BEHAVIORAL AND ENVIRONMENTAL CAUSES

Gene mutations and brain abnormalities that make a person more likely to develop BD, however, do not cause the disorder unless certain behavioral and environmental factors are also present. One behavioral factor that increases the risk for BD in genetically vulnerable people is substance abuse. Using alcohol, marijuana, cocaine, and other recreational drugs also makes BD worse in people who already have it. Scientists are studying marijuana's effects on BD extensively as more and more US states are legalizing the drug. Many health care professionals are concerned about its effects. Psychiatrist Chittaranjan Andrade writes that policy makers should view legalization trends "with concern" because studies show marijuana causes psychosis to develop two to three years earlier than it would have otherwise emerged in genetically susceptible people. Marijuana users who develop BD are also likely to develop rapid cycling and to experience serious cognitive problems. "Legislating marijuana into legitimacy does not make it safe," Andrade warns.[14]

Numerous environmental events have also been linked to an increased risk for BD. Some of the most common are traumatic events and stress, especially when they occur during brain development before or after birth. NIMH reported on several studies in 2018 that showed babies born to women with large amounts of inflammation or stress are more likely than normal to have brain damage in areas that regulate emotions, learning, and memory. This is because inflammation and stress involve the production of immune chemicals and stress hormones. These chemicals are known to damage a developing brain. Children who endure early trauma such as physical or sexual abuse are also likely to have large amounts of stress hormones in their bodies.

Bipolar disorder affects many people. Its exact causes are unclear, though genetics, behavioral factors, and environmental factors all contribute. With professional help, bipolar disorder can be successfully managed.

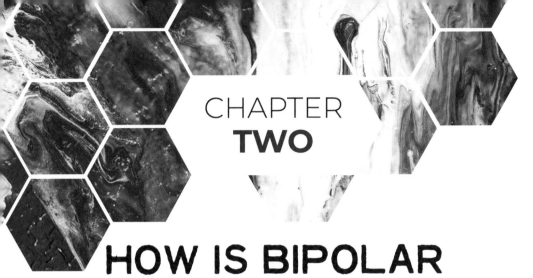

CHAPTER
TWO

HOW IS BIPOLAR DISORDER DIAGNOSED?

What is now known as bipolar disorder has been described throughout history, and symptoms and effects on people have remained remarkably consistent over time. In ancient times, people thought mental disorders came from possession by evil spirits or demons, or were a result of divine punishment. Some doctors in ancient times attributed BD-like diseases to biological factors, but this viewpoint did not become prevalent until the later decades of the twentieth century. Hippocrates, a physician who lived from around 460 BCE to 375 BCE in ancient Greece, is credited with being the first doctor to attribute disease to biological factors. He believed imbalances in the four so-called humors, or fluids, in the body caused sickness. These humors were blood, yellow bile, black bile, and phlegm. Hippocrates attributed melancholia, or depression, to excessive amounts of black bile. Although the concept of humors was later proved to be inaccurate, Hippocrates's revolutionary idea that biology caused disease was later confirmed.

Hippocrates was an ancient Greek physician who linked mental disorders with biological factors. Aretaeus, another ancient Greek physician, linked mania with depression.

All forms of mental illness were once called "madness." In 2 CE, the ancient Greek physician Aretaeus of Cappadocia wrote, "They with whose madness joy is associated, laugh, play, dance night and day, and sometimes go openly to the market crowned, as of victors in some contest of skill. . . . Others have madness attended with anger, and these sometimes [tear] their clothes and kill their keepers, and lay violent hands upon themselves."[15] His reference to "go openly to the market crowned, as of victors" illustrates his observation that "mad" people displayed evidence of psychosis.

Aretaeus was also the first known doctor to link mania and depression in a single disease: "I think that melancholia is the beginning and a part of mania. . . . The development of a mania is really a worsening of the disease (melancholia) rather than a change into another disease."[16] After Aretaeus wrote about melancholy and mania, the combination was not discussed much in medical circles until the late 1600s, when the Swiss physician Théophile Bonet wrote about a disease he called *manico-melancholicus*. In 1854, the French psychiatrist Jean-Pierre Falret published a detailed description of the disorder. He called it *la folie circulaire*, meaning circular insanity, because of its cyclical nature. Psychiatrist Emil Kraepelin named it manic-depressive psychosis in the early 1900s. In 1905, Swiss psychiatrist Carl Jung described patients with "occasional elation, exaggerated self-confidence, mental productivity . . . not sufficient to warrant a diagnosis of chronic mania . . . these are cases of a hypomanic state that cannot be regarded as psychotic."[17]

> "I think that melancholia is the beginning and a part of mania. . . . The development of a mania is really a worsening of the disease (melancholia) rather than a change into another disease."[16]
>
> – *Aretaeus the Cappadocian, a doctor in ancient Greece*

The disorder was later termed *manic depression* before receiving its present name in 1980. The evolving understanding of BD opened the door to psychiatrists establishing a variety of subtypes. The *Diagnostic and Statistical Manual of Mental Disorders, 5th Edition (DSM-5)* is the first *DSM* in which *Bipolar and Related Disorders* is its own category.

The number of people diagnosed with BD has changed dramatically over time. In particular, the numbers have vastly increased since 1990,

Diagnosing bipolar disorder is complicated. Health care professionals use a list of criteria to determine whether someone qualifies for a diagnosis.

but experts are unsure of why. Studies indicate that the increased number of cases has been especially pronounced in young people up to the age of nineteen. For example, the number of diagnoses in people in this age-group in the United States increased forty-fold, from 25 cases to 1,003 cases per 100,000 people between 1994–1995 and 2002–2003. The number of adults with BD increased from 905 to 1,679 cases per 100,000 people from 1994–1995 to 2002–2003. These numbers continued to increase during the first two decades of the twenty-first century. However, experts believe statistics kept by the Centers for Disease Control and Prevention (CDC) and the National Institutes of Health (NIH) underestimate the true number of people affected because only about half of those with BD are diagnosed.

A COMPLICATED PROCESS

The diagnostic process for BD is complicated and challenging for numerous reasons. The NIMH estimates that on average, people with BD wait up to ten years before receiving a correct diagnosis. One reason is that several other mental disorders share characteristics with BD, and misdiagnoses among these disorders are common. Two studies found that 40 percent of BD patients were misdiagnosed with major depression. A survey conducted by the National Depressive and Manic-Depressive Association found that 69 percent of respondents were initially misdiagnosed. More than one-third of them had to wait ten years or more for a correct diagnosis.

Diagnosis of ADHD became more and more common during the 1990s and early 2000s, and it continues to rise. The fact that it shared symptoms with BD, along with the fact that 60 to 70 percent of people with BD also have ADHD, increased the number of misdiagnoses of these disorders. "The rates of misdiagnosis and delayed diagnosis are particularly high among patients with bipolar symptoms; they are astronomical for patients with bipolar disorder plus ADHD," explains an article in *ADDitude Magazine*.[18] Both ADHD and BD include difficulty focusing and sitting still. But when a doctor follows a patient over time, it becomes easier to distinguish the two. ADHD does not include cycles of mania and depression, nor does it involve psychotic symptoms.

"The rates of misdiagnosis and delayed diagnosis are particularly high among patients with bipolar symptoms; they are astronomical for patients with bipolar disorder plus ADHD."[18]

– Roberto Olivardia, PhD

ANOSOGNOSIA AND DENIAL

Anosognosia, or the lack of awareness that one is ill, poses other challenges to diagnosis. Psychiatrist E. Fuller Torrey explains that this term comes from the Greek words *nosos*, meaning disease, and *gnosis*, meaning knowledge. "It literally means to not know a disease," he states, adding that anosognosia is caused by damage to the brain.[19] People who do not know they are ill see no reason to visit a doctor for a diagnosis. Studies indicate anosognosia affects approximately 40 percent of people with BD.

Denial is a closely related factor that can delay diagnosis. In this case, an individual is aware something is wrong but does not seek treatment because of fear, shame, or the perception that consulting a doctor shows weakness. Other times, an individual ignores or denies a diagnosis of BD. In either case, denial leads to worsening symptoms and negative effects on individuals and families. Joe, a man in his forties, just wanted the diagnosis of BD to go away. He refused to admit he was ill and would not take the medications his doctor prescribed. His wife dreaded his increasingly hostile and reckless behavior that included tormenting her with frightening notes and spending money he did not have. His fear of his diagnosis led him to avoid going to the doctor, even when a lump appeared on his neck. When he finally went to the emergency room because he was bleeding from the mouth, he was diagnosed with stage IV cancer. Though he did finally start taking his bipolar medication, he lost his life to the cancer. His wife, Kathleen, said, "His denial of reality was part of his illness. And that's why he died. It was as much the bipolar as it was the cancer that killed him."[20]

Delusions of grandeur, such as believing oneself to be a celebrity, can be a sign of a manic episode. Hypomanic people are less likely to have delusions of grandeur but may make grandiose statements, such as a non-writer planning to quit his job and write a novel.

John Budin, a New York City psychiatrist, denied being sick for many years after his bipolar symptoms began. Even though he had diagnosed and treated many people with BD in his job, he says, "It had never occurred to me that I, too, was ill." His denial led him to conceal his symptoms from everyone, including his wife. "For years, my bipolar closet door remained firmly shut. . . . I was living in a

"For years, my bipolar closet door remained firmly shut. . . . I was living in a castle with the drawbridge pulled up, wandering around by myself behind impenetrable walls."[21]

– Psychiatrist John Budin, who has bipolar disorder

30

castle with the drawbridge pulled up, wandering around by myself behind impenetrable walls." When he realized he had bipolar disorder, "I viewed myself as weak and pathological." What finally led him to accept and deal with his illness was the realization that by denying it, "we are confirming that we are worthy of shame."[21]

DIFFERENT PERCEPTIONS

Since distinguishing quirky or odd behavior from mental illness often depends on unclear, subjective factors, another reason for misdiagnosis or delayed diagnosis is that doctors, patients, and families may not have the same understanding of an individual's symptoms. Many psychiatrists and psychologists report that people with BD describe their behaviors, thoughts, and motivations differently than others describe them. This is one reason why clinicians like to speak with family members as well as with patients. A patient named Lauren, for example, stated that she often exercised for up to five hours per day, collapsed from exhaustion, and then left her three children with their grandparents because she believed her ex-husband and her mother did not help out enough. In contrast, Lauren's mother attributed Lauren's behavior to being selfish and irresponsible. The psychiatrist Lauren consulted about her exhaustion believed her symptoms reflected BD. Thus, different interpretations of Lauren's behavior could have delayed diagnosis or led to a different diagnosis had her psychiatrist not been the one who attributed her behavior to BD.

THE CONSEQUENCES OF A DELAYED OR INCORRECT DIAGNOSIS

The consequences of delayed diagnosis can be serious. "Bipolar disorder is a complex illness to manage, and its misdiagnosis results in further treatment complications," state psychiatrists Tanvir Singh and Muhammad Rajput in their study of misdiagnosis. "Initial misdiagnosis results in delay of appropriate treatment, which in turn increases the risk of recurrence and chronicity [having episodes all the time]."[22] People with BD who are initially misdiagnosed also spend more time in hospitals, have higher health care costs, and attempt suicide more often than those who are correctly diagnosed from the start.

A male patient had symptoms of BD since early childhood but did not receive a diagnosis because his parents did not take him to a doctor. He found out firsthand the effects of delaying diagnosis. "I've always had mood swings. I used to throw huge tantrums when I was a kid. As I got older, the highs got higher and the lows got lower. I lost several jobs and ruined a whole bunch of relationships. Finally, I decided nothing could be worse than living like I was, and I went to get some help," he writes.[23]

Widespread cases in which BD was misdiagnosed as major depressive disorder have revealed one of the most serious consequences of misdiagnosis. The antidepressant drugs used to treat depression can trigger previously absent episodes of mania and rapid cycling. More studies need to be conducted to determine which bipolar patients can safely take antidepressants.

A related impediment to a prompt and correct diagnosis is that many patients only complain and visit a doctor when depressive episodes occur. These individuals may feel great during manic episodes and thus see no reason to seek medical help. This phenomenon is known as the seduction of mania. When these patients do seek treatment, they often fail to mention that they also have manic episodes, so they are misdiagnosed with depression. This happened to Andy Behrman, who wrote the book

Electroboy: A Memoir of Mania in 2002. "I saw eight psychiatrists before I got my diagnosis and was misdiagnosed almost always with depression," he said in an interview with *bp Magazine*. "Back then, I thought they were all right. And it's understandable, because I only went to those doctors when I was in my down periods, feeling terrible. I didn't go when I was feeling elated or manic. And that's still a problem today: people who are bipolar are not so willing to give up their mania."[24]

THE DIAGNOSTIC PROCESS

Before making a diagnosis, a health care professional conducts a physical examination to rule out diseases that may be causing symptoms.

OVERDIAGNOSING BIPOLAR DISORDER

Some people who face a bipolar disorder misdiagnosis have the disorder but are not properly diagnosed. However, sometimes the opposite is true. This was the case for US Navy veteran William Royster. Royster joined the Navy as a pilot in 1986. In 1996, his plane was shot down during a training exercise. He was injured and honorably discharged from the Navy in 1997. Royster was treated for his injuries at the Kansas City Veterans Affairs (VA) Medical Center. In 1998, Royster became a commercial pilot for United Airlines. But in 2004, Royster's doctor recommended that he be evaluated for PTSD. Royster was diagnosed with bipolar II and told that he would not be able to work. He was medically retired from his job as a pilot and was treated for BD for ten years. In 2013, he met with a new psychiatrist. This doctor said he did not meet the criteria for bipolar II as he never had manic episodes. Royster filed a lawsuit for $35 million against the Kansas City VA. The lawsuit was ultimately dismissed due to being filed outside the statute of limitations.

Some studies have shown that overdiagnosis of BD can be just as problematic as underdiagnosis. A study conducted at the Rhode Island Hospital in Providence, Rhode Island, found that three times as many patients were overdiagnosed as were underdiagnosed. Mark Zimmerman, director of outpatient psychiatry at the hospital, said, "Whether bipolar disorder is more frequently overdiagnosed or underdiagnosed is not really important. Rather, it is critical that it is accurately diagnosed."

Mark Zimmerman, "Head to Head: Is Underdiagnosis the Main Pitfall When Diagnosing Bipolar Disorder? No," The BMJ, February 22, 2010. http://bmj.com.

This may include laboratory tests, such as blood tests and brain imaging tests. Although there are no brain imaging tests or blood chemistry tests that can diagnose BD, these tests can rule out conditions like brain tumors or hormone imbalances that may be causing symptoms.

The physician takes a medical history to find out what illnesses the patient and his family members have had. She talks with the patient and, if possible, with family members to learn about the patient's symptoms and behavior changes. Standardized questionnaires help doctors assess the patient's moods and behaviors. If a general practice doctor suspects the diagnosis is BD or another serious mental illness, she often recommends that the individual see a psychiatrist—a medical doctor who specializes in mental illness—for a diagnosis.

DSM-5 CRITERIA

A mental health professional ultimately diagnoses the illness using *DSM-5* or WHO's International Classification of Diseases, 11th Revision (ICD-11) criteria. The *DSM-5* has been used since 2013, and it refers to plural *bipolar disorders* to describe seven types of bipolar disorder. The most common types are bipolar I disorder, bipolar II disorder, cyclothymic disorder, and bipolar disorder-unspecified or other-specified.

A diagnosis of bipolar I is given when a patient has extreme manic episodes. Most people also experience depressive episodes, but this is not required for a diagnosis. A manic episode must last a week, during which the person is irritable or high-spirited for most days of the week. The person must also have at least three changes of behavior from a list that includes exaggerated self-esteem, talkativeness, a reduced need for sleep, a desire to do many things at once, and risky behavior. The changes in behavior must be noticeable by others and must cause

DIAGNOSING MANIC AND
DEPRESSIVE EPISODES

Diagnostic criteria for:

Manic Episodes	Depressive Episodes
One week of abnormally elevated, expansive, or irritable mood; and elevated levels of goal-directed activity or energy present for most of the day.	For a continuous two-week period, either a depressed mood or a loss of interest or pleasure.
At least three of the following: · Grandiosity or inflated self-esteem · Decreased need for sleep · More talkative than normal · Flight of ideas · Distractible · Increased psychomotor agitation, such as pacing or tapping toes · Excessive behavior with the potential for negative consequences	At least five of the following: · Depressed most of the day every day · Lower interest in usual activities nearly every day · Lower appetite · Inability to sleep or sleeping more than usual · Psychomotor agitation (such as pacing or tapping toes) or retardation (slowing down of physical movements and thought processes) · Fatigue or loss of energy · Feelings of worthlessness or guilt · Indecisiveness or difficulty thinking or concentrating · Thoughts of suicide

The *DSM-5* lists specific criteria for diagnosing someone with bipolar disorder. One major part of diagnosis is the presence of manic or depressive episodes. The *DSM-5* also includes criteria for diagnosing these episodes.

problems with school, work, or other responsibilities. A major depressive episode has different criteria. An episode must last for two weeks, and the person must have at least five symptoms from a list outlined in the *DSM-5*. This list includes intense sadness or despair, loss of interest in activities once enjoyed, feeling worthless or guilty, sleep problems, feeling restless or agitated, changes in appetite, loss of energy, frequent thoughts of death or suicide, and difficulty concentrating, remembering, and making decisions.

A person is diagnosed with bipolar II when he or she has at least one major depressive episode and one hypomanic episode. Hypomanic episodes are less extreme than manic episodes. Linda Logan, who was diagnosed with bipolar II, characterized hypomania as "mania with a tether."[25] Symptoms of hypomania are less severe than those of mania and only need to appear for four days for diagnosis. People with hypomania are often still able to function in a way that those with full mania cannot.

Another form of BD is cyclothymic disorder. It is diagnosed when a person has experienced hypomanic and depressive periods that do not fulfill official criteria for a hypomanic or depressive episode. Symptoms must last two years for adults to be diagnosed and one year for children and adolescents.

Other specified bipolar disorder includes symptoms that are consistent with BD but that do not fulfill criteria for diagnosing any particular bipolar or related disorder. Many children and adolescents are given this diagnosis. Mental health professionals emphasize that it is not a cop-out. They instead use this diagnosis to acknowledge that a patient has a mood disorder that should be followed to see how it develops over time. Other categories of diagnosis include substance/medication-induced bipolar and related disorder, bipolar and related disorder due to another medical condition, and unspecified bipolar and related disorder.

In addition to placing patients into a diagnostic category, doctors also rate the severity of the illness. The severity is ranked as mild, moderate, or severe. More than 80 percent of those diagnosed with BD in the United States have severe cases.

Diagnosing bipolar disorder is a complicated process. It is an important one, however. Having a proper diagnosis is a key first step for patients to get the treatment they need.

PRECISION PSYCHIATRY AND BIPOLAR DIAGNOSIS

In 2018, a group of researchers affiliated with universities worldwide published a study that emphasized the need for precision psychiatry in diagnosing and treating bipolar disorder. This model would separate bipolar disorder into various separate stages, just as many non-psychiatric illnesses are divided. This would benefit patients because it would allow physicians to precisely tailor diagnosis and treatment to a particular stage of illness.

For instance, studies show that many people with BD experience a very early stage, long before the first extreme symptoms appear. This stage often includes an elated mood, increased energy, and unyielding self-confidence. At that point, psychiatrists could analyze the person's family history, behaviors such as substance abuse, and experiences such as early sexual or physical abuse, all of which increase the risk for developing BD. Therapy that focused on changing BD-triggering behaviors and on developing coping skills to deal with unpleasant past events could then be implemented to help prevent full-blown BD. "While early stages of the disease might show a better response to simpler treatment regimens, chronic stages might need more complex treatments and still show less clinical improvement," the researchers write. Similar staging models have improved diagnosis and treatment in cancer and heart disease.

Estela Salagre et al., "Toward Precision Psychiatry in Bipolar Disorder," Frontiers in Psychiatry, September 2018. www.ncbi.nlm.nih.gov

CHAPTER
THREE

WHAT IS LIFE LIKE WITH BIPOLAR DISORDER?

Life with bipolar disorder is challenging for patients and their families because it affects many aspects of existence, including the ability to think, interact with others, and work. It also affects life expectancy. People with BD have a much lower life expectancy than those without the disorder. Studies show that starting in adolescence, they have twice the risk of dying from heart disease, three times the risk from lung disease, four times the risk from murder, and fourteen times the risk from suicide. The stresses associated with BD and the fact that many patients smoke cigarettes and abuse recreational drugs underlie these increased risks from physical disease. Risky physical activities or behavior associated with mania can also shorten life expectancy.

Overall, experts say that there are several ways patients can improve their quality of life. Finding a support group, taking their medications, and regularly visiting a psychotherapist are all important steps. They can also engage in activities that reduce stress. A 2017 study by clinical

Mania can cause people to act in ways they normally wouldn't. After a manic episode, people might be embarrassed by their actions.

psychologist and researcher David J. Miklowitz and his colleagues supports these ideas. The researchers found that a small amount of cognitive impairment and an ability to minimize depressive episodes are the strongest predictors of living well with BD. They defined living well as having the ability to keep a job, do well in school, and maintain rewarding personal relationships.

The challenges of living with BD begin before diagnosis and continue for the rest of patients' lives. Before seeking treatment, patients struggle with decisions about whether or not to do so because of anosognosia, stigma, and other factors. Those who choose to seek help may react to their diagnosis in different ways.

REACTIONS TO DIAGNOSIS

Many patients say receiving a correct diagnosis is a relief. A diagnosis identifies the cause of their symptoms and helps their doctors implement appropriate treatment. Those who were repeatedly misdiagnosed tend to be especially relieved. A correct diagnosis, states one patient, "was a huge breakthrough for me. . . . I now had words to explain what I was going through. . . . For the first time in a long time, I am learning to deal with my feelings, emotions and moods."[26]

Others, however, are devastated by a diagnosis of BD, and some try to pretend nothing is wrong. Martha, who was hospitalized and diagnosed with bipolar I at age thirty-four, denied her illness because she knew nothing about BD. She called the diagnosis "this death sentence" and asked her doctor why he considered her normally straightforward, blunt personality to be a mental disorder.[27] However, once her care team helped her find a local support group, she learned from other patients that denial is not helpful and changed her way of thinking. "I've learned to accept that I've got something biochemical that goes haywire, but it's not the sum total of who I am," she states.[28]

> "I've learned to accept that I've got something biochemical that goes haywire, but it's not the sum total of who I am."[28]
>
> – Martha, who has bipolar disorder

Patients who are knowledgeable about BD may also struggle to accept the diagnosis because of conflicts with their self-perception. Psychiatrists note that such conflicts often arise from grief similar to the grief people feel after losing a loved one. According to Ellen Frank, a professor of psychiatry at the University of Pittsburgh, patients and their families become overwhelmed with grief over losing the person who

Some people diagnosed with bipolar disorder struggle with accepting their illness. Others struggle to define their identity as separate from their disorder.

existed before the disorder entered his or her life. Frank refers to this as the "lost healthy self."[29] Learning to reconcile one's core self with the new role as a patient with a mental illness can take time, and different patients go about it in different ways. Some reacquaint themselves with the core self and develop a plan to fit the disorder into their thoughts, behaviors, and lifestyle.

A NEW SELF

A female patient who struggled to redefine her identity as separate from her disorder found it took a while to be comfortable with her new self. "I feel like everything I do now is somehow connected to my being sick. If I'm happy, it's because I'm manic. If I'm sad, it's because I'm depressed.

I don't want to think that every time I have an emotion, every time I get angry at somebody, it's because I'm ill. . . . People say I'm a different person every day, but that's me! I've never been a stable person," she says.[30]

"I feel like everything I do now is somehow connected to my being sick. If I'm happy, it's because I'm manic. If I'm sad, it's because I'm depressed. I don't want to think that every time I have an emotion, every time I get angry at somebody, it's because I'm ill."[30]

– A female bipolar patient

Some patients do the opposite of trying to separate the self from the disorder and over-identify with it, instead. In other words, they think BD crushed their pre-illness identity, meaning they become their disorder. One woman stated that she knew no men would ever ask her for a date because she was now bipolar. Her doctor noted that she seemed to forget she was still a person with other positive attributes and dimensions. Indeed, psychiatrists state that patients who over-identify with BD may distance themselves from familiar positive roles such as being a good student, a competitive athlete, or a parent. Patients who identify strongly with a new manic identity may overspend, going into massive debt. Conversely, identifying strongly with a depressive identity may lead them to skip school or work.

Some patients, particularly those with severe psychosis, are unaware of how or when BD hijacks their identity. For example, Kay Jamison did not become aware that her bipolar selves were different from her true personality until her episodes subsided. She had always liked old-fashioned things, including elegant, classic furniture and architecture. But during a long-lasting manic episode, she rented an apartment in an ultra-modern building and bought ultra-modern furniture. When the episode ended, she did not know where the piles of past-due bills and receipts in her apartment came from. Looking at them, she writes, "was like going on an archaeological dig through earlier ages of one's mind."[31]

STIGMA AND BIPOLAR DISORDER

Stigma tied to BD further affects patients' challenges with identity and ability to cope with their disorder. Stigma related to mental illness is not a new phenomenon. When society thought demonic possession caused madness, affected people were put in insane asylums to keep them away from others. Many were also beaten and tied up for being evil.

Forcibly isolating people with mental illness continued after the demonic possession theory disappeared, mostly because of the persistent viewpoint that mental illness reflects a weakness of character. Affected people hoped evidence that biological factors cause disorders like BD would diminish stigma, but this did not happen. One study found that "stigma toward BD is ubiquitous and has insidious consequences for affected individuals and their families."[32] Stigma was present in families and individuals, work and school environments, social situations, and the health care industry.

> "Stigma toward BD is ubiquitous and has insidious consequences for affected individuals and their families."[32]
>
> – From "Stigma and Bipolar Disorder: A Review of the Literature" by Lisa D. Hawke et al.

PERCEPTION, CONSEQUENCES, AND STIGMA

The stigma surrounding BD comes from prejudices and incorrect perceptions of why people with BD feel and behave the way they do. Stigma and patients' fears about the perceptions of others influence

Mania can cause people to behave recklessly, such as gambling excessively. This can contribute to stigma.

their decisions from the time they are first diagnosed. After diagnosis, an immediate concern is whether or not to tell family, friends, coworkers, and others. Many patients fear that revealing their diagnosis may result in being fired from a job, being shunned by friends and loved ones, being discriminated against when trying to buy or rent a home, or even having one's children taken away.

Government agencies say the purpose of removing children from homes in which a parent or other caregiver has BD or another mental illness is to keep these children safe from destructive behavior.

However, many people with BD believe those who enforce these agencies' laws and rules allow their own prejudiced notions and the stigma related to BD to taint their assessments. Sometimes, even if children in a home seem fine, social workers and others assigned to assess the situation seem to look for proof that a parent with BD cannot take care of them, according to numerous patients. This is why many do not share their diagnosis.

In other cases, people with BD simply find others' well-intentioned but ignorant and stigmatizing remarks to be degrading and hurtful, so they do not share their condition with anyone. When one woman was diagnosed with BD after being misdiagnosed repeatedly, she viewed the correct diagnosis as an opportunity to finally do something constructive about her symptoms. But after she told friends, family, and coworkers about the diagnosis, she found their remarks disheartening. While some were supportive, some were ignorant or hurtful. She disliked such remarks as "You don't seem crazy," "Maybe you're just imagining it," "You don't need medication," and "Just think positive." One person said, "You didn't seem like you had bipolar until you were diagnosed." The author's response was, "This one hurts a lot. I have finally, for once in my life, had my feelings and emotions validated. I understand better why I am the way I am, and for the first time, I can actually work towards a proper plan to treat it, or minimize it. . . . This response completely crushes that feeling."[33]

In many cases, people with BD internalize stigma that stems from linking the disorder with a weakness of character or with evilness, and they start to think and act like someone who is emotionally and cognitively weak and worthy of contempt. This contributes to many instances of self-harm and suicide. One study estimates that between 25 and

45

WHY IS BIPOLAR DISORDER SO HIGHLY STIGMATIZED?

Stigma is directed at people with all forms of mental illness, but studies show that bipolar disorder is particularly stigmatizing. This partly results from media portrayals of people with mania as violent, out-of-control, and raving. News stories about someone with BD committing a serious crime reinforce the stigma. According to an article in *Current Psychiatry*, approximately 60 percent of people with bipolar I also deal with substance abuse in their lifetime. This worsens stigma because many in the public have little sympathy for those they view as too lazy and weak to control this behavior.

In addition, reports by the US Department of Justice show 18 percent of inmates in federal and state prisons and 25 percent in local jails in the United States have BD, making it the second most common mental disorder among prisoners after major depression. Studies indicate that inmates with BD are likely to clash with prison officials and to commit acts of violence against other inmates and prison guards. After being released from prison, most end up being reincarcerated for other crimes.

60 percent of people with bipolar disorder will attempt suicide in their lives. It estimates between 4 and 19 percent will die by suicide. Actress Ricki Lake's ex-husband, Christian Evans, had BD. After he killed himself in 2017, Lake told *People* magazine that Evans's final act represented the fact that he "didn't want to be labeled as bipolar" and could no longer fight the label.[34]

CONSEQUENCES OF BIPOLAR BEHAVIOR

The consequences of bipolar behavior often stem from differences in perception. Families may believe their loved one with BD lies in bed all day because she is inconsiderate, irresponsible, too lazy to go to school or work, too selfish to care about dragging her own family into poverty, and too weak to pull herself out of her bad mood. In contrast, the person with BD may lack the insight to understand the cause or nature of certain unhealthy behaviors. All she knows is that she is overwhelmed with sadness and hopelessness and has no energy. One man with BD stated that his legs felt like they were encased in concrete and his brain struggled to emerge from drowning in deep water when he was depressed.

In some cases, a consequence of bipolar behavior is that families and friends cut the person with BD out of their lives because they fear him or do not understand his behavior. In thirty-four-year-old Kevin's case, his mania caused him to believe that grandiose investment plans were going to lead to vast riches. Kevin convinced his father to lend him money for this investment, which Kevin invested recklessly. After Kevin lost most of the money, his angry siblings wouldn't speak to him. Kevin's father had planned to help Kevin move out and become independent. But instead, he told Kevin to repay every lost dollar before he would help.

Many patients report that they also encounter stigma or discrimination from medical professionals. Kay Jamison, for example, was hurt and angry when her doctor spoke to her in a manner she found degrading and upsetting. This doctor asked if she planned to have children, and she responded that she would like to do so. He then asked whether she would continue to take her bipolar medications while pregnant, and she started to explain why she would. The doctor interrupted, she later wrote: "At that point, in an icy and imperious voice that I can hear to this day, he stated . . . 'You shouldn't have children.' . . . I felt sick, unbelievably and utterly sick, and deeply humiliated."[35]

Some health practitioners who treat pregnant women and deliver babies refuse to accept patients with disorders like BD. They have concerns about the fact that some medications used to treat BD are not considered safe for use during pregnancy. Some of these drugs can cause birth defects. These concerns also affect people with BD.

People with bipolar disorder can make poor financial decisions. This can cause tension in families.

"I'm terrified of having children," states Emma, a twenty-five-year-old woman with bipolar II. "I would have to be off my medication at least during pregnancy, if not longer if I breastfeed. Beyond actually having a child, raising a child is scary. I would hate for my bipolar to affect my relationship with them negatively."[36] Other women say the risk of passing on gene mutations that increase the risk of BD to a baby is also frightening.

DOES MANIA HAVE AN UPSIDE?

Despite the challenges of living with BD, numerous medical experts, historians, and patients themselves point out that many exceptionally creative, brilliant people have been classified as mentally ill to some degree throughout history. In the fourth century BCE in ancient Greece, for instance, the philosopher Aristotle made one of the first widely known connections between creativity, melancholia, and mania. "Why is it that all those who have become eminent in philosophy or politics or poetry or the arts are clearly of an atrabilious [related to bile] temperament, and some of them to such an extent as to be affected by diseases caused by black bile?" he asked in his book *Problemata*.[37]

Emma, the twenty-five-year-old with bipolar II, takes issue with this stance. She finds it upsetting when individuals, the media, and others refer to the genius and productivity of those with mania:

> I feel like the thing Hollywood gets the most wrong about living with bipolar disorder is that mania is a super power or gift. I'm thinking about artists that created while manic, or Carrie [Claire Danes's character] on *Homeland* cracking the case because of wild leaps in logic while manic. The idea that the world deserves the results of mania more than those with bipolar disorder deserve safety in their own minds is really [upsetting]. It drives me crazy, this attitude that mania is a gift that justifies the pain of depression. . . . My manias are my most destructive times, both in terms of how it affects my life and my relationships.[38]

> "I feel like the thing Hollywood gets the most wrong about living with bipolar disorder is that mania is a super power or gift."[38]
>
> – *Emma, a twenty-five-year-old woman with bipolar disorder*

Most people with BD say the challenges in living with the disorder would diminish if more people understood what these challenges entail. In the meantime, many simply echo Gabe Howard's plea: "Treat us the same as you would everyone else, because we are just like everyone else."[39]

CHAPTER
FOUR

HOW IS BIPOLAR
DISORDER TREATED?

T hroughout history, treatment for BD reflected health care providers' understanding of the disorder's causes. Most treatments before the development of modern medicine consisted of religious or medical exorcism to drive out evil spirits. Other solutions included trepanation (removing part of the skull) and bloodletting (releasing so-called bad blood with leeches or other methods).

Hippocrates, who attributed mood disorders to excessive amounts of black bile, suggested eating a healthy diet to restore the correct balance of humors and to thus cure the illness. "Let food be thy medicine and medicine be thy food," he wrote.[40] Some doctors in ancient Greece and Rome also advised patients with mania or melancholia to soak in a bath containing lithium salts or to drink spring water, which also contained lithium. Lithium calmed mania and diminished depression. However, it was largely forgotten after the collapse of the Greek and Roman empires until its rediscovery in the late nineteenth century. Lithium is used in pill form in modern times. Another form of treatment emerged during the

Many people manage their bipolar disorder with a combination of therapy and medication. Patients work with health care professionals to figure out what works best.

fifth century CE, when the first insane asylums opened. Doctors began treating madness by locking patients up to prevent them from hurting others and themselves.

MODERN TREATMENT

Modern treatment for BD is individualized for each patient and reflects the prevailing view that it is preferable to allow patients to live in the community rather than being confined to a hospital. When necessary, patients are temporarily hospitalized to stabilize them during acute episodes. Health care professionals later follow up with outpatient care.

Modern treatments also reflect the consensus that biological, social, environmental, and behavioral factors cause BD. Health care professionals consider appropriate medications to be the primary treatment element because they stabilize mood, reduce symptoms, and increase the individual's ability to function in home, work, and social settings. Experts say optimal treatment also includes psychotherapy, which enhances patients' ability to cope and live well with the disorder and makes them more likely to take prescribed medications.

In most cases, BD treatment is ongoing and requires lifelong maintenance, even during times when patients have few or no active symptoms. Studies prove that regularly taking medication decreases the number and severity of new episodes. In addition, the earlier treatment begins, the less chance there is that symptoms and brain damage will worsen. This is the reason doctors are so interested in making treatment plans easier to access and stick to. As mental health staff at the Mayo Clinic write, "Bipolar disorder doesn't get better on its own."[41]

> "Bipolar disorder doesn't get better on its own."[41]
>
> *– Mayo Clinic staff*

TREATING BD WITH MEDICATION

There are five main types of medication for BD. They include lithium, anticonvulsants, antipsychotics, antidepressants, and anti-anxiety medications. Patients may be prescribed one type of medication, or they may take more than one. Patients sometimes need to try several medications before finding one that works. The most commonly used mood stabilizer is lithium. It is effective in approximately 60 percent of the

Lithium has been used to treat a variety of illnesses. Before lithium's use in mental health, people visited hot springs containing the mineral for its health benefits.

people who take it and helps decrease the number of manic episodes they experience. Lithium is also known to reduce the risk of suicide. However, it is rarely effective for patients with rapid cycling and mixed states. Additionally, patients may experience unpleasant side effects. Side effects may include drowsiness, dry mouth, nausea and vomiting, weight gain, brain fog, acne, joint and muscle pain, kidney damage, and tremors. It can be difficult for doctors to find dosages that are strong enough to do what they are supposed to do without side effects. It is also important for doctors to carefully monitor blood levels of lithium and other medications to ensure the dosages are not strong enough to cause life-threatening damage to the body.

Scientists are just starting to understand how and why lithium is effective. It has been widely used since its rediscovery in 1871 and its subsequent surge in popularity after the Australian doctor John Cade publicized its effects in 1949. Before its use in the mental health field, lithium saw other medicinal uses. It was present in many mineral springs and used in 1847 by a London man to treat gout, a form of arthritis caused by uric acid in the blood. When the kidneys do not excrete enough uric acid, it can create sharp crystals in the joints, resulting in the pain and swelling of gout. It was in 1871 that lithium was first prescribed as a treatment for mania by William Hammond. Hammond was a professor of Diseases of the Mind and Nervous system at Bellevue Hospital Medical College in New York. A doctor in Denmark wrote about using lithium to treat melancholic depression in 1894. After this, however, there was little mention of lithium in psychiatric writing. Cade had read about lithium's use for gout and wondered if uric acid might also cause mania. He began using it to treat his patients and wrote of his success. This caused others to study lithium, and its use in psychiatry grew. Edward Shorter, a professor of medicine, calls lithium the most effective psychiatric treatment besides electroconvulsive shock therapy.

ANTICONVULSANT MEDICATIONS

If lithium is not effective, or if its side effects are unbearable, patients are often prescribed another mood stabilizer. One category of medications commonly used to treat bipolar disorder is known as anticonvulsants. These medications are used to treat seizures, but they are also effective in treating bipolar disorder. One example is valproic acid, also called valproate. Doctors find valproate works as well as lithium for controlling manic episodes and works better than lithium for mixed states and rapid cycling. Some people find valproate easier to tolerate than lithium.

Some take both valproate and lithium. Anticonvulsants can still cause side effects. Some of these include nausea, weight gain, dry mouth, and skin rashes.

ANTIPSYCHOTIC MEDICATIONS

Patients who experience psychosis may also take an antipsychotic such as risperidone, which mostly diminishes psychosis, mania, and mixed states. Some patients use risperidone for long-term control, but for others, it mostly helps control immediate traumatic episodes. Andrew, age fifteen, developed severe hallucinations and delusions that led him to become suicidal and harm himself. He was hospitalized and given risperidone, which had unpleasant side effects such as weight gain, drooling, muscle twitches, and extreme fatigue. He called it "a pair of handcuffs for the mind." But he soon realized the drug saved his life. "Risperdal gave my mind a chance to recover. It put the brakes on the psychotic episode which ultimately gave me an opportunity to take back control of my life," he stated.[42]

Like many medications used to treat BD, antipsychotics are better at controlling mania than depression. However, studies published in 2019 by psychiatrist Lakshmi N. Yatham and his colleagues at the University of British Columbia found that a newer antipsychotic called cariprazine, which the Food and Drug Administration (FDA) approved for treating mania in 2015, also effectively treats depression in people with bipolar I. The researchers

> "Risperdal gave my mind a chance to recover. It put the brakes on the psychotic episode which ultimately gave me an opportunity to take back control of my life."[42]
>
> – Andrew, age fifteen, who has bipolar disorder

Some people are hesitant to take medications due to possible side effects. It's important to talk to a health care professional before stopping a prescribed medication.

found that cariprazine has fewer and less serious side effects than most antipsychotics.

ANTIDEPRESSANTS

Another type of drug that many patients take is antidepressants. However, antidepressants work best to treat major depression, and their effectiveness at treating BD is controversial in the health care community. Since antidepressants can also trigger manic episodes in people with

BD, many doctors hesitate to prescribe them. In addition, certain antidepressants can trigger suicidal behavior in adolescents, so doctors often avoid prescribing them for people in this age-group. Patients who do use an antidepressant usually take one in a class of drugs called selective serotonin re-uptake inhibitors (SSRIs). These drugs, such as Prozac and Zoloft, act by increasing the amount of serotonin or other neurotransmitters in the brain.

ANTI-ANXIETY MEDICATIONS

Anti-anxiety medications called benzodiazepines can sometimes be prescribed as a short-term treatment for BD. Examples include Xanax, Klonopin, and Valium. Benzodiazepines are fast-acting and slow the activity of the brain, making them helpful for treating mania. However, they can be habit-forming and addictive.

NONCOMPLIANCE WITH DRUG REGIMENS

Many of the medications commonly used to treat BD have unpleasant side effects. Side effects affect different people differently, and some experience mostly physical side effects, such as nausea or joint pain. Others experience more mental side effects, such as brain fog and difficulties remembering things. Linda Logan, for example, noted that the lithium and other drugs her doctor prescribed "turned my formerly agile mind into mush."[43] She could not think clearly or remember things, and she felt no emotion. Other patients may have both types of side effects.

Many times, adjusting dosages or the time of day when patients take their medications can diminish or eliminate the side effects. However, this is not always true, and in other cases it takes months or even years for doctors to find the right combinations and dosages. Many patients stop taking their medications for these reasons.

However, more than just side effects keep people with BD from taking medications. Studies indicate that up to half of BD patients stop taking their medications. The most common reasons are anosognosia and medication side effects. In addition to common side effects such as dizziness and nausea, patients can find more noticeable side effects such as muscle tremors that are unbearable or embarrassing. Experts note that stopping medication can be dangerous due to the potential for severe fluctuations in mood, risk-taking behavior, and worsening of symptoms. "Avoid stopping medication without talking to your doctor first," NIMH advises.[44]

> "Avoid stopping medication without talking to your doctor first."[44]
>
> *– The National Institute of Mental Health*

One possible side effect of BD medication is a condition called tardive dyskinesia (TD). TD is a condition that causes uncontrollable muscle spasms, especially in the face. It can be caused by some antipsychotic medications and lithium. Unlike many patients, Shelly Barber did not let embarrassment about TD lead her to stop her drug regimen. She shared the events that embarrassed her and her method of dealing with them in an article she wrote for her fellow BD patients. Once, she recalled, she sang with a group in a Christmas video recorded at her church, and her husband later said "it looked like I was doing the chicken dance in my chair! My hands moved like a locomotive. It was pretty embarrassing."[45] However, she learned to laugh at herself and to not worry about what others thought, because she knew her medications helped her live well with BD.

The allure of mania can also affect patients' decisions to stop taking their medications. Patients often report enjoying the euphoria of manic episodes. As such, they resist medications that alter their elevated mood states. The desire or need to recapture the euphoria and the perception that they can accomplish anything leads many to risk the dangerous, out-of-control manic episodes and crushing depression that result from discontinuing their prescribed medications. This was what happened to Kay Jamison about six months after she started taking lithium, even though as a psychiatrist, she knew she should not stop. "I had become addicted to my high moods," she wrote.[46]

PUBLIC SAFETY VERSUS PATIENT RIGHTS

Controversies exist over forced treatment and hospitalization for people with BD or other mood disorders who pose a danger to themselves or others. In 1999, an unmedicated schizophrenic man pushed a woman named Kendra under a subway train in New York. This case led to Kendra's Law, which permits courts to order people to take their medications regularly to prevent being forcibly hospitalized and medicated.

Psychiatrist E. Fuller Torrey notes that forced hospitalization and medication are necessary when patients are unaware they are ill (anosognosia) or when psychotic delusions convince them others will harm them. Torrey also argues for forced treatment for humane reasons. "The failure to treat such individuals often leads to homelessness or incarceration," he states. "On humane grounds alone, is it fair to leave those who are not aware of their own illness living in the streets and eating out of garbage cans, as over 25 percent of the population with severe mental illness do?"

In contrast, Judi Chamberlain co-founded the National Empowerment Center. She fought against forced medication and hospitalization for mentally ill people like herself until her death in 2010. Her main argument was that people affected by a mental disorder have the right to be and act as they choose.

Dr. E. Fuller Torrey, "Impaired Awareness of Illness: Anosognosia," Mental Illness Policy Org., n.d. https://mentalillnesspolicy.org

There are many varieties of psychotherapy. Psychotherapy and medication are often used together to manage symptoms of bipolar disorder.

OTHER MEDICAL TREATMENTS

Some patients are not helped by any of the drugs used to treat BD. In such cases, doctors may perform electroconvulsive shock treatment. It consists of doctors administering electric shocks to a sedated person. These shocks cause a convulsion that often helps people with serious mental disorders by causing chemical changes in the brain.

Electroconvulsive treatment is often used in severe cases involving suicidal thoughts or psychotic symptoms. It is recognized as a safe, effective technique in these cases. However, it does carry some side effects, including short-term memory loss, confusion, nausea, and headaches.

PSYCHOTHERAPY

Psychotherapy is another proven treatment that helps regulate BD. It can be administered

"I had become addicted to my high moods."[46]

– Psychiatrist and bipolar patient Kay Jamison

one-on-one with a patient and therapist, or in a group. Many patients and their families also participate in family therapy sessions. Psychotherapy is used in conjunction with appropriate medications.

In his book *The Bipolar Disorder Survival Guide*, Miklowitz explains one factor that drives the success of modern psychotherapies: "It is now considered good clinical practice to have people with bipolar disorder (or their relatives) weigh in on major decisions about their treatment."[47] Previously, psychiatrists and therapists were likely to tell patients what they should do, without the patient's input. More collaborative approaches increase patients' willingness to follow doctors' orders because they actively participate in the details. The type of therapy used depends on a patient's needs. The most common forms are cognitive behavioral therapy, social rhythm therapy, and family therapy.

COGNITIVE BEHAVIORAL THERAPY

Cognitive behavioral therapy (CBT) involves a therapist helping a patient develop new ways of thinking. One way in which this helps patients cope and live fuller lives is that CBT helps them analyze and sort out issues with self-identity. Experts say this is important because learning to distinguish one's identity from BD is important. CBT also helps people learn to identify the early signs of new episodes. This ability allows people to take action to prevent full-blown episodes. For example, if a patient who has always been introverted and rarely enjoys socializing suddenly starts going to parties every night, this is a clear indication that a manic episode is brewing. The patient would learn to pause and notice these signs in order to take precautionary action. A bipolar patient may also notice that she feels angry, aggressive, or overly energetic with no need for sleep, and this can alert her that mania is taking over. When families participate in therapy, each family member can learn about how to help the patient detect and take action to prevent full-blown episodes, such as encouraging him to take a walk outside if arguments with relatives commonly trigger episodes.

Neuroscientists have used brain imaging to identify some of the biological underpinnings for the success of CBT. Studies show the brain circuits that regulate emotions overlap with those that regulate cognition. This means new ways of thinking can lead patients to implement new ways of responding to emotional situations. "Over the long-term, frequent use of reappraisal leads to enhanced control of emotion, interpersonal functioning, and psychological and physical well-being," explains a study led by clinical psychologist and neuroscience researcher Philippe R. Goldin.[48] Goldin's team used fMRI scans to determine that reappraising a situation that generates negative emotions increases activity in areas of the prefrontal cortex that underlie cognitive control of emotions. It also reduces activity in parts of the brain that process emotion and self-perception.

INTERPERSONAL AND SOCIAL RHYTHM THERAPY

Ongoing participation in the psychotherapy technique known as Interpersonal and Social Rhythm Therapy (IPSRT) is also known to help

Having a support group is key to managing bipolar disorder. Family-Focused Therapy can help family members learn how to best support a loved one with BD.

patients deal with current episodes, cope better with BD over time, and prevent relapses by adding stability to their lives. The method was designed to help patients deal with disruptions in daily routines that can compound stress and trigger episodes. The IPSRT technique teaches patients to implement behaviors that promote what Ellen Frank calls "stable biological rhythms." These include consistent sleep-wake cycles and other consistent routines like being on time for school, work, or other events. Implementing stable routines stabilizes chemicals throughout the body that respond to internal bodily processes called circadian rhythms. Frank explains that all people can experience tiredness and disorientation from disruptions in regular routines. IPSRT is effective because it helps patients establish consistent rhythms in all aspects of their lives. In addition, "IPSRT often helps patients accept the lifelong nature of their illness, reduces the denial commonly associated with the disorder, and thus facilitates medication adherence," Frank notes.[49]

FAMILY-FOCUSED THERAPY

Family-Focused Therapy (FFT) works well for many patients of all ages and their families. Miklowitz co-created and tested FFT with his colleagues at UCLA during the 1990s and early 2000s. These professionals observed that patients with families that are educated about BD and that strive to communicate respectfully experience far better outcomes than those without supportive families. FFT programs include calculating a score called *expressed emotion*, or EE. EE quantifies the ways in which family members and caregivers of people with mental illness speak to these individuals. According to Miklowitz, "a relative is considered 'high EE' if he or she expresses a high number of critical comments, makes one or more statements of hostility, or shows emotional overinvolvement (i.e., overprotective, exaggerated emotional responses, or inordinate self-sacrifice) when describing interactions involving the patient."[50] Studies show that patients whose relatives routinely express criticism, hostility, and contempt have more episode relapses, more hospitalizations, and less overall satisfaction and productivity in life. One goal of FFT is to lower EE scores, as a lower EE is associated with a better prognosis.

FFT involves a set number of sessions—usually either twelve or twenty-one, depending on individual needs—in which therapists first provide education about causes, symptoms, treatments, and other aspects of BD. The educational phase also trains families and patients to identify stressors and early signs that an episode is developing. For example, sixteen-year-old Jenna regularly experienced increased irritability and started sleeping less when one of her mixed-state episodes was brewing. Her therapists taught her to keep a daily mood chart to help her identify these early signs when they occurred. They also helped her identify specific events that triggered these early signs, since these events often resulted in Jenna exploding with rage, destroying items in her family's home, and threatening to harm her mother and brother. Jenna learned that these events included arguments with her family or friends and increased amounts of schoolwork.

During the next phase of FFT, Jenna learned to speak respectfully to family members and to engage in productive brainstorming to devise solutions to the arguments or other issues. At the same time, the therapists helped Jenna's mother realize that she often spoke to Jenna in a critical manner and antagonized Jenna by yelling about Jenna's poor choice of friends. After the therapy was completed, everyone in the family thought things were much improved. They also knew they could come back for refresher sessions when needed.

After treating thousands of bipolar patients and their families, Miklowitz sums up his findings about FFT by stating, "It is my strong belief that people who do best with the disorder are those who have learned to recognize triggers for their mood cycles and learned how to minimize the impact of these triggers."[51]

> "It is my strong belief that people who do best with the disorder are those who have learned to recognize triggers for their mood cycles and learned how to minimize the impact of these triggers."[51]
>
> – Psychologist David J. Miklowitz

CELEBRITIES WITH BIPOLAR DISORDER

Many celebrities with bipolar disorder have spoken out about the disorder to reduce stigma. One early advocate was Carrie Fisher, who played Princess Leia in the Star Wars movies. Fisher was diagnosed with bipolar disorder when she was twenty-nine. She was one of the first female celebrities to open up about her diagnosis, paving the way for others to do the same. She fought against mental illness stigma until her death in 2016. In her 2008 memoir, she wrote, "At times, being bipolar can be an all-consuming challenge, requiring a lot of stamina and even more courage, so if you're living with this illness and functioning at all, it's something to be proud of, not ashamed of. They should issue medals along with the steady stream of medication."[1]

Singer and actress Demi Lovato is another star who has opened up about her struggles. Lovato was diagnosed with bipolar disorder when she went to rehab in 2011. She said her diagnosis was a relief because she could work to treat the disorder. She became the spokesperson for an initiative called Be Vocal: Speak Up for Mental Health. "I knew that there were two options: I could either not talk about my stint in rehab and hope that it went away, or I could talk about it and inspire people to get help for their issues, as well, so that's exactly what I did,"[2] Lovato said. Other stars who have spoken out about their bipolar diagnoses include Mariah Carey, Russell Brand, and Catherine Zeta-Jones.

1. Quoted in Jessica Migala, "Eight Times Carrie Fisher Shattered the Stigma on Mental Illness," Health.com, December 28, 2016. http://health.com.

2. Quoted in Christina Heiser, "Demi Lovato Speaks Up About Living with Bipolar Disorder," Women's Health, May 28, 2015. http://womenshealthmag.com.

INFORMAL MEASURES

Many people with BD also join online or in-person support groups with other people going through similar challenges. Such connections enhance patients' and families' awareness of episode triggers and help them learn from others who live with the disorder.

Mental health experts say patients should also incorporate components of a healthy lifestyle that apply to everyone. These include eating a healthy diet, exercising regularly, not smoking, not using alcohol or recreational drugs, getting enough sleep, and learning to cope with

Actress and writer Carrie Fisher was diagnosed with BD when she was twenty-nine. She was an outspoken voice against mental health stigma until her death in 2016.

stress using techniques such as meditation, yoga, tai chi, or simply chatting with a friend. Psychologist Russ Federman says avoiding alcohol and recreational drugs is especially important: "If you want to live well with bipolar disorder, then drugs and alcohol don't factor into the equation."[52]

STILL MORE TO DO

Despite the positive effects of many modern treatments, BD is still one of the most severe, disabling mental disorders, and it is tied to premature death from a variety of physical causes, as well as suicide. Researchers are thus conducting many studies to improve diagnosis and treatment and to hopefully develop methods to prevent BD. Besides searching for

Patients with bipolar disorder play a more active role in their treatment today than they typically have in the past. This helps patients find the best treatment to manage their symptoms.

new drugs, researchers are exploring new uses for established drugs used to treat other illnesses. For example, ketamine was originally used as an intravenous anesthetic during surgery, and it has recently proved to be effective as a nasal spray that quickly relieves severe depression in people with BD. However, concerns over patients abusing the drug have prevented widespread use.

The complexity of emotional, cognitive, and physical issues and challenges surrounding treatment for BD reflect the complexity and diverse nature of the disorder and the individuals who live with it. Some with BD hate themselves and view the disorder as a curse that completely ruined their lives. Some are grateful that medications allow them to live fulfilling lives. And some, like those connected with organizations like the Mental Patients' Liberation Front and the National Empowerment Center, believe they have the right to not be medicated if they so choose.

As a psychiatrist and individual with BD, Kay Jamison understands more about her disorder than many other patients do. Yet when asked whether or not she would choose to have BD if she could make such a choice, her response reflected the complexity of everything surrounding BD. "If lithium were not available to me, or didn't work for me, the answer would be a simple no," she writes. But since it does help her, she states, her answer is yes. "I honestly believe that as a result of [bipolar disorder] I have felt more things, more deeply; had more experiences, more intensely; loved more, and been more loved; laughed more often for having cried more often; appreciated more the springs, for all the winters," she explains.[53]

One thing many modern BD patients agree upon is that trends toward giving affected people more say in their treatment decisions and other aspects of the disorder is a positive development. Patients now serve on university research review boards, so their input is considered in determining which research projects are funded. In addition, the overall emphasis among doctors and patients is shifting from the goal of treatment being eliminating all symptoms to instead being designed to help patients cope and achieve their personal goals despite the challenges BD presents. "I firmly believe that people with bipolar disorder lead happier lives when they do not carry the expectation that recovery means being free of all symptoms," Miklowitz writes in his discussion of this trend.[54] Instead, he states, viewing recovery as the ability to live well with the illness helps more people find fulfillment and happiness.

SOURCE NOTES

INTRODUCTION: THE CHALLENGES OF BIPOLAR DISORDER

1. Marcia Purse, "Living with Bipolar Disorder," *Verywell Mind*, September 14, 2019. www.verywellmind.com.

2. "Bipolar Disorder," *National Alliance on Mental Illness*, August 2017. www.nami.org.

3. Gabe Howard, "Facing the Stigma and Stereotypes of Bipolar Disorder," *WebMD*, November 20, 2017. www.webmd.com.

4. Paul J. Harrison et al., "Innovative Approaches to Bipolar Disorder and Its Treatment," *Annals of the New York Academy of Sciences*, April 25, 2016. www.ncbi.nlm.nih.gov.

5. Frederick K. Goodwin and Kay Redfield Jamison, *Manic-Depressive Illness: Bipolar Disorders and Recurrent Depression*, Second Edition. New York: Oxford University Press, 2007, p. xix.

CHAPTER 1: WHAT IS BIPOLAR DISORDER?

6. "Bipolar Disorder," *National Institute of Mental Health*, April 2016. www.nimh.nih.gov.

7. John Budin, "John Budin," *Depression and Bipolar Support Alliance*, n.d. www.dbsalliance.org.

8. Kay Redfield Jamison, *An Unquiet Mind*. New York: Vintage Books, 1995, p. 38.

9. Linda Logan, "The Problem with How We Treat Bipolar Disorder," *New York Times*, April 26, 2013. www.nytimes.com.

10. Medifocus, *Medifocus Guidebook on: Bipolar Disorder*. Silver Spring, MD: Medifocus, 2011, pp. 50–51.

11. Jamison, *An Unquiet Mind*, pp. 36–37.

12. Jennifer H. Barnett and Jordan W. Smoller, "The Genetics of Bipolar Disorder," *Neuroscience*, November 24, 2009. www.ncbi.nlm.nih.gov.

13. "First Stem Cell Study of Bipolar Disorder Yields Promising Results, U-M and Prechter Fund Scientists Say," *Heinz C. Prechter Bipolar Research Program*, March 25, 2014. http://medicine.umich.edu.

14. Chittaranjan Andrade, "Cannabis and Neuropsychiatry, 2: The Longitudinal Risk of Psychosis as an Adverse Outcome," *Journal of Clinical Psychiatry*, 2016. http://psychiatrist.com.

CHAPTER 2: HOW IS BIPOLAR DISORDER DIAGNOSED?

15. Quoted in Francis Adams, *The Extant Works of Aretaeus, the Cappadocian*. London: Printed for the Sydenham Society, 1856, p. 302. *Internet Archive*. http://archive.org.

16. Quoted in Jules Angst and Andreas Marneros, "Bipolarity from Ancient to Modern Times: Conception, Birth and Rebirth," *Journal of Affective Disorders* 67 (2001) 3–19. http://academia.edu.

17. Carl C. Jung, "On Manic Mood Disorder," *International Association for Analytical Psychology*, n.d. https://iaap.org.

18. ADHD Editorial Board, Janice Rodden, and Roberto Olivardia, PhD, "The Physician's Guide for Distinguishing Bipolar Disorder and ADHD," *ADDitude Magazine*, September 25, 2019. http://additudemag.com.

19. E. Fuller Torrey, "Impaired Awareness of Illness: Anosognosia," *Mental Illness Policy Org*, n.d. http://mentalillnesspolicy.org.

20. Kathleen Maloney, "Life with Joe, Before and After His Illness," *HuffPost*, September 4, 2014. www.huffpost.com.

21. Budin, "John Budin."

22. Tanvir Singh and Muhammad Rajput, "Misdiagnosis of Bipolar Disorder," *Psychiatry*, October 2006. www.ncbi.nlm.nih.gov.

23. "What Now?" *Depression and Bipolar Support Alliance, South Florida Chapter*, n.d. http://dbsasouthflorida.org.

24. Quoted in Sara Solovitch, "The Shocking Tale of Andy Behrman," *bphope*, Summer 2005. http://bphope.com.

25. Logan, "The Problem with How We Treat Bipolar Disorder."

CHAPTER 3: WHAT IS LIFE LIKE WITH BIPOLAR DISORDER?

26. "How Invalidating My Bipolar Disorder Invalidates Me," *National Alliance on Mental Illness*, n.d. http://nami.org.

27. Quoted in David J. Miklowitz, *The Bipolar Disorder Survival Guide*, Third Edition. New York: Guilford Press, 2019, pp. 16–17.

28. Quoted in Miklowitz, *The Bipolar Disorder Survival Guide*, Third Edition, p. 24.

29. Ellen Frank et al., "Interpersonal and Social Rhythm Therapy: An Intervention Addressing Rhythm Dysregulation in Bipolar Disorder," *Dialogues in Clinical Neuroscience*, September 2007. www.ncbi.nlm.nih.gov.

30. Quoted in Miklowitz, *The Bipolar Disorder Survival Guide*, Third Edition, p. 80.

31. Jamison, *An Unquiet Mind*, p. 75.

SOURCE NOTES
CONTINUED

32. Lisa D. Hawke et al., "Stigma and Bipolar Disorder: A Review of the Literature," *Journal of Affective Disorders*, September 5, 2013. www.sciencedirect.com.

33. "How Invalidating My Bipolar Disorder Invalidates Me."

34. Quoted in Julie Jordan, "Ricki Lake Reveals Her Ex-Husband Died by Suicide Amid Battle with Bipolar Disorder: 'I Wanted to Save Him.'" *People*, March 1, 2017. http://people.com.

35. Jamison, *An Unquiet Mind*, p. 191.

36. Quoted in Tessa Miller, "This Is What It's Actually Like to Live with Bipolar Disorder," *Self*, December 1, 2017. www.self.com.

37. Quoted in Michael Heyd, *Be Sober and Reasonable: The Critique of Enthusiasm in the Seventeenth and Early Eighteenth Centuries*. Leiden; New York: E.J. Brill, 1995, p. 96.

38. Quoted in Miller, "This Is What It's Actually Like to Live with Bipolar Disorder."

39. Howard, "Facing the Stigma and Stereotypes of Bipolar Disorder."

CHAPTER 4: HOW IS BIPOLAR DISORDER TREATED?

40. Quoted in Richard Smith, "Let Food Be Thy Medicine . . . ," *BMJ*, January 24, 2004. www.ncbi.nlm.nih.gov.

41. Mayo Clinic Staff, "Bipolar Disorder," *Mayo Clinic*, January 31, 2018. http://www.mayoclinic.org.

42. Andrew, "Taking Risperidone to Treat Psychosis: Andrew's Story," *HeadMeds*, October 3, 2018. www.headmeds.org.uk.

43. Logan, "The Problem with How We Treat Bipolar Disorder."

44. "Bipolar Disorder," *National Institute of Mental Health*.

45. Shelly Barber, "How to Deal with Bipolar's Involuntary Body Movements," *bphope*, n.d. www.bphope.com.

46. Jamison, *An Unquiet Mind*, p. 98.

47. Miklowitz, *The Bipolar Disorder Survival Guide*, Third Edition, p. 1.

48. Philippe R. Goldin et al., "The Neural Bases of Emotion Regulation: Reappraisal and Suppression of Negative Emotion," *Biological Psychiatry*, March 15, 2008. www.ncbi.nlm.nih.gov.

49. Ellen Frank et al., "Interpersonal and Social Rhythm Therapy: An Intervention Addressing Rhythm Dysregulation in Bipolar Disorder."

50. David J. Miklowitz et al., "Family-Focused Treatment for Bipolar Disorder in Adults and Youth," *Journal of Clinical Psychology*, May 2007. www.ncbi.nlm.nih.gov.

51. Miklowitz, *The Bipolar Disorder Survival Guide*, Third Edition, p. viii.

52. Russ Federman, "Alcohol, Drugs and Bipolar Disorder: A Bad Combination," *Psychology Today*, October 11, 2010. www.psychologytoday.com.

53. Jamison, *An Unquiet Mind*, p. 218.

54. Miklowitz, *The Bipolar Disorder Survival Guide*, Third Edition, pp. 4–5.

FOR FURTHER RESEARCH

BOOKS

Andrea Balinson, *Depression, Anxiety, and Bipolar Disorders*. Broomall, PA: Mason Crest, 2018.

Sherri Mabry Gordon, *Coping with Bipolar Disorder*. New York: Rosen Publishing, 2020.

Andrea C. Nakaya, *What Is Bipolar Disorder?* San Diego: CA, ReferencePoint Press, 2016.

H.W. Poole, *Bipolar Disorder*. Broomall, PA: Mason Crest, 2016.

Rachael Rothman-Kerr, *Bipolar Disorder: Dealing with Mania and Depression*. New York: Lucent Books, 2019.

INTERNET SOURCES

Russ Federman, "Alcohol, Drugs and Bipolar Disorder: A Bad Combination," *Psychology Today*, October 11, 2010. www.psychologytoday.com.

David B. Feldman, "The Tragedy of Mental Illness Stigma," *Psychology Today*, August 10, 2018. www.psychologytoday.com.

Linda Logan, "The Problem with How We Treat Bipolar Disorder," *New York Times*, April 26, 2013. www.nytimes.com.

Tessa Miller, "This Is What It's Actually Like to Live with Bipolar Disorder," *Self*, December 1, 2017. www.self.com.

WEBSITES

American Psychiatric Association (APA)
www.psychiatry.org

The APA is a professional organization for psychiatrists, and its website also offers information for the public, including details about diagnosis, symptoms, treatment, research, living with disorders, and issues that affect doctors, patients, and families. The APA publishes the *DSM-5* for psychiatrists and provides information about issues and changes in diagnostic criteria and how this affects patients.

Depression and Bipolar Support Alliance (DBSA)
www.dbsalliance.org

This nonprofit organization offers support to people and families affected by bipolar disorder and major depression. The website contains information about diagnosis, prevalence, symptoms, treatment, research, stigma, living with bipolar disorder, and where and how to obtain medical, social, and peer support, along with comments and articles written by patients and families.

National Institute of Mental Health (NIMH)
www.nimh.nih.gov

NIMH is a US government agency that is part of the National Institutes of Health, which sponsors medical research and informs the public about health and sickness. The NIMH website offers detailed information on all aspects of mental health, including bipolar disorder statistics, diagnosis, symptoms, treatment, and research.

INDEX

INDEX
CONTINUED

IMAGE CREDITS

Cover: © fizkes/Shutterstock Images

5: © Antonio Guillem/Shutterstock Images

6: © New Africa/Shutterstock Images

8: © Rawpixel.com/Shutterstock Images

11: © Antonio Guillem/Shutterstock Images

13: © fizkes/Shutterstock Images

15: © milicad/Shutterstock Images

18: © pixelheadphoto digitalskillet/Shutterstock Images

22: © monticello/Shutterstock Images

25: © Luis War/Shutterstock Images

27: © Monkey Business Images/Shutterstock Images

30: © Sergey Kurbatov/Shutterstock Images

35: © Red Line Editorial

39: © mooremedia/Shutterstock Images

41: © cheapbooks/Shutterstock Images

44: © Blackday/Shutterstock Images

48: © Iakov Filimonov/Shutterstock Images

51: © Vgstockstudio/Shutterstock Images

53: © Niwat panket/Shutterstock Images

56: © Seksan.TH/Shutterstock Images

60: © Freeograph/Shutterstock Images

63: © Twinsterphoto/Shutterstock Images

67: © Featureflash Photo Agency/Shutterstock Images

68: © Photographee.eu/Shutterstock Images

ABOUT
THE AUTHOR

Melissa Abramovitz is an award-winning author and freelance writer who specializes in writing educational nonfiction books and magazine articles for all age-groups, from preschoolers through adults. She has published hundreds of magazine articles and more than fifty educational books for children and teenagers. She also writes short stories, poems, picture books, and materials for writers. Melissa graduated *summa cum laude* from the University of California, San Diego, with a degree in psychology and is also a graduate of the Institute of Children's Literature.